M000170242

WHEN CHURCH HURTS

WHEN CHURCH HURTS

Richelle Milson

ISBN (Paperback): 978-1-7781650-2-3
ISBN (Hardback): 978-1-7781650-0-9
ISBN (Digital): 978-1-7781650-1-6

Front Cover Design: Kamar Martin
Photographer: Atalia's Photos
Book Interior: The Ready Write-Her

Unless otherwise listed, scripture quotations are taken from the Holy Bible, New Living Translation, copyright ©1996, 2004, 2015 by Tyndale House Foundation. Used by permission of Tyndale House Publishers, Carol Stream, Illinois 60188. All rights reserved.

Also contains scriptures from, *The Holy Bible: New King James Version.* (1982). Thomas Nelson.

Printed in the United States of America.

First printing edition 2023.

DEDICATION

This book is dedicated to my son Shawn who when I told him I was writing a book was excited and always pushed his mother to write daily. I got annoyed a few times, but he was consistent. So, I say thank you to my handsome son. Remember you can do ALL THINGS!

To anyone and everyone who has experienced any type of church hurt. I want you to know that I empathize with you and although your story may be different from what I experienced or shared just know that God loves you and He sent His only begotten son Jesus to die on the cross for you. Get the healing you need and reconnect back to God if you have not already. As they say, "The church is a hospital," and we all need to see the doctor for something. That doctor is Jesus Christ. Build that relationship with Him and find a family of believers that will love you and not hurt you.

- Nuff Love, Ri

TABLE OF CONTENTS

INTRODUCTION

Hey y'all, my name is Richelle but y'all can call me Ri. Thank you for purchasing this book as I'm sure in one way or another you may have experienced some type of church hurt. It's a topic that MANY brush under the rug and one that I find we don't talk enough about. I was directed by the Holy Spirit to write a book. He gave me the title for another book a few years back while attending Heather Lindsay's Pinky Conference in Atlanta with my girl, whom I truly admire, Sarah Jakes Roberts. When I say I was wrecked, I was wrecked! My BF and I left that conference so filled and confident in what direction God was leading us. My God!!!

My prayer and hope, as I share what I have experienced, is that this would lead those with similar experiences back to a place where they can feel safe within the church. I hope and pray that you develop a stronger personal relationship with God the Father, knowing that He loves you oh so much and He sees everything. I want you to know that no matter what happens within any physical setting, you're still able to remain unmovable by the actions of man and stay connected to God. Jesus didn't come to earth for nothing. He is the best example of what it's like to have people love you one day and then hate you the next. But He still showed love, forgave, and completed His assignment on this earth. May you fulfill and complete your assignment and be healed fully in Jesus' name!

As I have grown, I have learned that the church is the body of Christ, as we read in scripture, and that each of us has a part to play. In 1 Corinthians 12:12-27, the Apostle Paul likens the body of Christ to our physical bodies.

> For as the body is one and has many members, but all members of that one body, being many, are one body, so also is Christ. For by one Spirit we were all baptized into one body-whether Jews or Greek, whether slaves or free-and have all been made to drink into one Spirit. For in fact the body is not one member but many. If the foot should say, "Because I am not a hand, I am not of the body? And if the ear should say, Because I am not an eye, I am not of the body," is it therefore not of the body? If the whole body were an eye, where would be the hearing? If the whole were hearing, where would be the smelling? But now God has set the members, each one of them, in the body just He pleased. And if they were all one member, where would the body be? But now indeed there are many members, yet one body. And the eye cannot say to the hand, "I have no need of you." No, much rather, those members of the body which seem to be

weaker are necessary. And those members of the body which we think to be less honorable, on these we bestow greater honor; and our unpresentable parts have greater modesty, but our presentable parts have no need. But God composed the body, having given greater honor to that part which lacks it, that there should be no schism in the body, but that the members should have the same care for one another. And if one member suffers, all the members suffer with it; or if one member is honored, all the members rejoice with it. Now you are the body of Christ, and members individually.

We read that the body has many members and within that, each has a significant role in fully functioning and operating in the fullness as God has designed it. Ephesians 4:16 reminds us that the whole body is joined and held together with each part doing its unique special work.

The physical church often puts emphasis on one body part more than the other. For instance, let's take the office of the prophet, which God has appointed and placed within the church. However, it appears as if this gift to the body has been used, abused, and misused as anyone can prophesy and/or give a word. As with any other gift, the goal is to always build the church. The office of the prophet will carry a strong hatred for the devil and comes to destroy and uproot things that are ungodly. They will carry compassion for the things of God and His people to warn, encourage, direct, bless, and edify the body of Christ. They are representatives in communicating God's word through speech, song, art, and/or written words. Many won't like a true prophet, but they are needed to bring correction.

What I have seen is that so many are hungry for a prophetic word from a man/woman and are quick to sow a seed, (or be manipulated into sowing), neglecting to check the fruit of the so-called prophet, and not testing the spirit of the word given. Don't get me wrong, there are some honorable men and women of God. However, I've decided to talk about this office because the word of God tells us that many false prophets will rise up in the end times, which we are vastly seeing. Due to the high volume of sowing a seed for every word given, (aka paying for a prophecy), many have lost their trust in the men/women of God because of this type of abuse. This then affects the entire body because it leads to a distrust in receiving messages from the Lord.

We are a part of one body with one mission which is to do the great commission. "And He said to them, "Go into all the world and preach the gospel to every creature. He who believes and is baptized will be saved, but he who does not believe will be condemned," (Mark 16:15-16). We are here to serve our Lord and Savior and win souls for our Heavenly Father's Kingdom by sharing the great news. Yet, there's so much division amongst the body that it is very annoying and can be a turn-off to anyone, from new believers to "seasoned saints," to anyone in between. I find it interestingly funny how Christians are the only ones who do not act and flow together. You can take any other religion and if you say the slightest thing, they will all rise up and fight for what they believe. You generally don't see the same with Christians. Many don't and won't fight back but are quick to fight each other about stuff like Saturday vs Sunday for worship.

Let's get into it some more, let one believer within a "house" leave and go to another church. It becomes a WWE match or a war of words of "you're wrong for leaving" etc. They straight out treat that individual as dirt, scum, and even as the BIGGEST sinner that ever lived. Some have been lied on horribly. I've witnessed and experienced it. Unfortunately, I even lost dear friends because of this nonsense - I sometimes questioned if they were really "dear friends." I don't know, it is what it is.

Y'all remember in the book of Corinthians when Paul was speaking about a false prophet? That is when we have every right to speak up against these "types of people." However, in many situations, this is not the case. I know anointed men and women of God who have been mistreated by the body of Christ within the physical church. I know some who have stepped down from ministry assignments and those who have left a ministry and then returned because of "faulty promises" to only once again be mistreated. I wonder how those who are new to the faith feel when they are still learning about the things of Christ, yet looked down upon because of the way they are dressed or may not know or use "church lingo." I'm far from perfect but *WE*, collectively as the body of Christ, have got to do better in how we treat the souls entrusted to us. Let me say this: WE DO NOT OWN ANY SOULS! THEY ALL BELONG TO CHRIST JESUS. And last I checked none of us were brutally beaten to the point of not being recognized or died on the cross for anyone's sins. So how dare the body of Christ act in such a manner of entitlement.

My prayer is that we all will learn, grow, and heal. I pray through the help of the Holy Spirit, we will serve as we are all called to do and really invest in people's lives. Many are hurt, broken, taxed out, and have nothing left all because of what they've experienced from a previous church body or what they have seen entering in as a new soul. Genuine investment is key, not that fake investment because people want large numbers on paper or the appearance of having a full house on camera for social media purposes, (yes, I said it), or even to get that offering because a particular individual or family is wealthy.

These are just some of the things I personally witnessed and experienced. I've been grieved, disappointed, hurt, you name it. I thank God for healing. Even writing this book has brought healing and allowed me to continue to always check myself not through my lens but through the lens of the Holy Spirit. I pray that we will begin to talk about Church hurt in a healthy manner and deal with these real issues that are occurring more frequently, including things that I didn't mention. I pray that we can grow and do away with any manipulation and fake love and truly display the love of our Lord and Savior to truly fulfill the Great Commission so that when Jesus returns for His church it will be one without spot or wrinkle. Amen!

CHAPTER 1
Distinguishing Between Seasons & Cycles

We all go through seasons, just like we have four seasons in weather, we as believers will go through this in our lives. The Bible speaks of seasons in Ecclesiastes 3:1-8, 11, (NLT):

> To everything there is a season, A time for every purpose under heaven: a time to be born, And a time to die; A time to plant, And a time to pluck what is planted; A time to kill, And a time to heal; A time to break

down, And a time to build up; A time to weep, And a time to laugh; A time to mourn, And a time to dance; A time to cast away stones, A time to embrace, And a time to refrain from embracing; A time to gain, And a time to lose; A time to keep, And a time to throw away; A time to tear, And a time to tear, and a time to sew; A time to keep silence, And a time to speak; A time to love, And a time to hate; A time of war, And a time of peace. Yet God has made everything beautiful for its own time. He has planted eternity in the human heart, but even so, people cannot see the whole scope of God's work from beginning to end."

We constantly need to be in tune with the Spirit of the Living God, so we know exactly what season we are in which could be joy, sadness, increase, or success for example.

Basically, I like to link this to our mindset. Often certain seasons can relate to how one feels or thinks. For example, during the winter season, some people may feel depressed. This is often linked to the lack of sun and fresh air due to being indoors which can often lead to a frame of mind that is constantly overthinking or worrying. In contrast, in the summer some feel happier because of the brightness of the outdoors and the warm sun causing their mindset to be one that is easy and peaceful.

Through scripture, we read, "Let this mind be in you which was also in Christ Jesus," Philippians 2:5. But what is the mind of Christ? The mind of Christ is to be able to discern spiritual things and operate as Christ did, selflessly. It is important that we also have a renewed mindset so that when we do experience the different seasons of life that will come as tests and trials or times of happiness and sadness, we will be able to respond accordingly. During those times we will need to be still in God and have a strong mindset. We need a mind that is focused, that does not doubt, that is not double-minded, and a mind that even during the most difficult times will still hold onto the promise of God. That mindset will help us to navigate through each season we will experience, allowing us to be strengthened in all the lessons that life will teach us.

As believers, we will go through many things that should lead us to draw closer to Him instead of turning away. Even though the building where we attend service is called the church, let us not forget that we as the body of Christ make up the church. It has many parts to it and each member is important. I don't care if you're called to clean the mirror in the bathroom, YOU ARE OF GREAT VALUE! Our goal is to win souls, not subtract from the body of Christ. No longer can we downplay or look down on individuals. There's so much emphasis on certain spiritual gifts and little effort on working with someone to develop character or walking with them through their deliverance process. What I have also witnessed is a heavy focus on talent. A person may sing well and be related to the pastor but have a nasty attitude, yet no one dares speak out against it because of the individual's relationship connection and overall talent. I have even witnessed one person being "sat down" because of open sin, such as becoming pregnant out of wedlock, but yet seen the other participant walking freely. Again, all because of the nature of certain relationship connections.

I believe it is vitally important that we use our God-given gifts and talents for His glory; however, don't just appoint just anyone based on looks. (I'm certain that unfortunately, you've seen favoritism in this area even in the church). People are chosen for positions based upon how well a person may speak and/or whom they are connected to even though they lack character, spiritual training and discipline, or just straight up have not been called. Let's not even talk about attending a prophetic fivefold ministry church and all you literally see each week is the same individuals or couples being prophesied over. I mean, huh? I remember serving under a leader and word got to him that a model had attended a few past services. When she returned again, it was a big spectacle to make sure that the model was taken care of. I was in disbelief that there were faithful members attending regularly and serving, yet there was no care for them when they had a need that could be physically met.

Just thinking of these things leads me to reflect on the words of a leader I once served with. "Talent can take you far, but character is what keeps you." Selah.

CHAPTER 2
Aren't YOU a Christian?

L et me tell you how this title came to be. One day, I was at one of my sister-friend's houses getting my hair done and another friend joined us. You know how us ladies are when we get together doing hair and chatting. We started talking about a wedding one of my sisters attended. It was a "real" Christian wedding - both the bride and groom were believers. At some weddings, despite the couple being believers they would play secular music but at a "Christian" wedding you will not hear any of that.

At one point some reggae came on and a few Christian folks were dancing. Many people were offended by the music, and of course, the most famous question came out "Aren't you Christian?" After rolling our eyes and a few "really's," I shared a similar story while I was at a wedding and began to sing a song that was being played during the reception. Old boy sitting next to me sees me in my zone, you know how we get when that old track comes on eyes closed singing with passion with your whole chest like you wrote the song. I then get asked, "Aren't you Christian?" As I was taken out of the lovely moment, I looked him in his eyes and said, "Yes, and just because I'm singing a song doesn't mean I'm not a Christian nor does it mean I can't enjoy myself at a wedding!!"

Wait, wait I got one more story. I was at work talking with a few other ladies, amped about an upcoming Jay-Z concert. Now before you start judging me, I was still a newbie in Christ and going through a mini turn away from Christ moment. Yes, I was in rebellion, let's call it what it was, Amen! Hence, me going to a Jay-Z concert. Anyway, one of my co-workers turned and said, "Aren't you a Christian?"

Man, what a famous line to always be asked as a believer, "Aren't you a Christian?" It's asked for anything! And I do mean anything - if you get angry, discuss a point back, wear some type of attire that's not a long dress, get tattoos, wear certain types of jewelry, fellas' earrings, wear makeup, have a weave, get colored hair, I mean we can go on and on. Who can relate? Yes, we are to demonstrate a lifestyle that is Holy unto God, and yes definitely show modesty, but who ever said any of those things weren't Christianly? At some point during your walk, I'm sure you have been asked or maybe you yourself have asked or said, "Aren't you Christian?"

I will definitely say that we do need to guard our gates, our ears and eyes, with what is being poured into us. A lot has changed with the music genres where the once hidden messages are now right in front of our faces. . The enemy is in every music video, song, movie, and even at concerts. Even if you're not completely aware of things going on in the spiritual realm, there are some things that you should be able to look at and think, "that's not ok." The question is, what are you doing about what you are almost being programmed, conditioned, and desensitized to?

I recall vividly being a rebellious Christian at a particular hip-hop concert. (Y'all I was a Hip Hop head let me tell you). As I was beginning to understand the spiritual realm more, I remember feeling so out of place and praying that nothing crazy happened. The atmosphere felt heavy and there was a clear difference between light and darkness. Although I knew I should have and could have left, I wanted to be there, so I remained. As the concert went on there was a moment when everything went completely black and everyone began doing the same thing, chanting the artist's name and throwing up the hand gesture. I knew within myself that it wasn't right, especially having an understanding of symbols and speaking words coming into agreement, I felt it was such a mockery, it was people worshiping the artist.

Let's also talk about artists who have made the decision to follow Christ, such as Kanye West, and the way most of the church responded and reacted. Like, did y'all forget that we were all in sin and that we had and/or may still have some type of struggle? Some of us had real support around us that helped and prayed for us through situations where we can stand stronger today. I wonder if anyone considers that because of who Kanye is, perhaps his circle around him could possibly be filled with yes men and opportunists. I say this to say, we should be praying for the lost, and continue praying for those who decide to follow Christ Jesus. The enemy hates us believers. We need to remember that everyone's path will be different. Our job as believers, no matter how far along you are in your walk, is to pray, cover in love, and show others the way through the word of God.

To those dabbling in music please be aware of what you are listening to. There are so many hidden messages within the music that many have been in a sense deaf too. Music at that time and prior had been a struggle of mine. God did bring me through and deliver me from a lot. I will admit that there are certain artists I will not entertain in my presence. However, I do still listen to some old-school music. I continue to pray and ask God for help and guidance in this area because He created music to worship Him. Yes, there are various genres of gospel music and gospel hip-hop has certainly helped a lot of us who love hip-hop music, but we can't be fooled because not all gospel music is of God. So let us all continue to ask God for His divine wisdom in this area. Amen.

CHAPTER 3
Why Y'all Always Judging Us?

We can agree that Christians get judged way more by EVERYONE. We will get the red flag if we voice our opinions. If we share that we don't agree with a particular lifestyle RED FLAG. We will even get judged or questioned by our fellow Christian brothers and sisters all because we are different denominations, RED FLAG. Ooop, let's not forget if we worship on a Sunday and not a Saturday or vice versa, RED FLAG. Can we get into tattoos and clothing RED FLAG!!! Lol, Ooooh I know I just pressed a button on some religious folks.

But guess what, Me nuh business, (for my non-Jamaican/West Indian folks I just said I don't care), but seriously there's so much more to be concerned about especially as we see what's happening during these last days that is being played out before us. Anyway, all that
I have mentioned I have been given a red flag on. I'm sure there are many more that you have experienced that if we were to check the Bible, there's not one book, chapter, or verse to explain the foolishness we see.

I'll tell you a story. I was on my way home from work one afternoon on the train when an older gentleman approached me. He didn't appear to be that much older than me, but I could tell he was a few years my senior, mind you I was 36 at that time. So ol' boy began engaging in conversation. I'm like whatever let's hear what he gotta say. He began casually asking about my day and making small talk. Then, he upfront asked if I'm a woman of God, so I said "Yea I'm a believer." He immediately tells me, "You're not." So I said, "Excuse you?" If you know me, you know the tone that came with this question, the one that's higher than my normal pitch and range, and I intently looked him square in his eyes. He continued on to say that by looking at me, he could tell that I was not a believer because I was wearing pants and had on makeup. Wait…. Wait… Wait…. What… (insert laughter, raised eyebrow, confused face here). So because I'm wearing pants and I'm wearing makeup, which was very light that day because I didn't normally wear makeup to work but that day I did. Shoutout to all the beautiful queens who wear makeup to enhance our beautiful God-given beauty. There's nothing wrong with wearing makeup as long as you are not using it as a cover-up to hide away from insecurities or it's being used as a vise. The use of it shouldn't be a reason why anyone feels the need to belittle someone making them feel less than others, which is what the man did. He made it seem as if I was going to hell because I wore pants and had on makeup …RED FLAG. Oh dear. Why do Christians and non-believers feel that if a person looks a certain way, says, or speaks a certain way that it's fair to question our Christianity?

Okay, I get it according to the word, John 15:19 says, "If you were of the world, the world would love its own. Yet because you are not of the world, but I chose you out of the world, therefore the world hates you." Or 1 John 2:15, "Love not the world, neither the things that are in the world. If any man loves the world, the love of the Father is not in him." We as believers are to bring back those that have wandered away from the truth. However, the Bible also says in John 7:24, "Do not judge according to appearance, but judge with righteous judgment."

Just because someone may "look" a certain way to you does not give you any right to automatically judge them and accuse them. We can't look at someone and say they're not a Christian because they wear this or that. You might not know that the same individual you are looking down on and judging may have had a crazy life B.C (before Christ) and here they are. Let's keep in mind that many have had interesting lives before being saved. Even in the way one "speaks." I've had "new believers" chat with me and got so excited that they slipped out a cuss word and immediately apologized. I do not look down on them. I work with them and just remind them to be mindful of their language, respectfully. As a Christian, I know it took some time for me to go through changes. It's a beautiful thing to witness how a person once was and see their growth over time. I used to sell weed and drink like crazy but now I've been transformed by the Holy Spirit and blessed to have some really great individuals who invested in my growth. I also try my best to work with people and be there to support and encourage them through their growth processes by letting them know they have a big sis available.

Galatians 6:1-3 says, "Brethren, if a man is overtaken in any trespass, you who are spiritual restore such a one in a spirit of gentleness, considering yourself lest you also be tempted. Bear one another's burdens, and so fulfill the law of Christ. For if anyone thinks himself to be something, when he is nothing, he deceives himself." Again, if a fellow brother or sister is caught in a transgression there is a way to correct them, love on them, and work with them. Some may need that extra support while they go through life as a new believer. You know how it is when you're going through that phase where you have one foot in and one foot out, still wanting to participate in a worldly lifestyle. I believe having real, open, and honest conversations from a non-judgmental place about our experiences and how we struggled and overcame will encourage any believer. I know those things helped me when I first began my walk with Christ, during my "wildin' out" period, and even now. It helps to have someone I can talk to about working out this Christian walk. Let us continue to show more grace to build our fellow brethren.

CHAPTER 4
Soooo, I Guess We Ain't and Can't Be Cool No More?

While in lockdown due to the pandemic, God gave me the idea to talk to various individuals about their life's journeys. We were all inundated with so much negativity daily, I wanted to share something positive and uplifting. I began "My Life's Journey with Ri," an online ministry that debuted on IG (Instagram) Live on Tuesday nights. The show is about giving glory and honor to God as we reflect on our life's journey and share experiences before knowing Christ, while knowing Him, and our present circumstances. It is a space where my guests can share their testimonies – the real, raw, and authentic stories – to give encouragement to others and let them know they are not alone on this faith walk. Just FYI, "My Life's Journey with Ri" is in its 3rd season and airs on Mondays at 8:30 PM EST, on IG Live and YouTube! To God be all the glory. I encourage you to check it out!

Back to the story at hand … when I first started the show, I reached out to someone who still attends a church I am a former member of. Everything was all good and we were still cool, at least I thought we were. The individual agreed to join me on IG Live and it seemed they were happy as they thanked me for thinking of them. I must admit I was hesitant to ask anyone from that place of worship because they seemed to treat those who had left as if they were working for the kingdom of darkness, by influencing the remaining members not to communicate or be in any type of relationship with that person. In spite of that feeling, I let fear die and gained the boldness to ask. I was excited as they agreed to join in sharing their journey.

Two weeks prior I decided to do something a little new and do a promo of the next 4 speakers I would have as my guest. I had messaged a friend of mine sharing how hesitant I was to do a post but asked the individual to join me in prayer that nothing would go left with the one guest. Meaning that no influences would speak or say anything negative regarding them joining me and that they would see this as something to build the kingdom. Within one hour of praying, I received the cancellation, stating they didn't have "peace" about it and wouldn't be doing the IG Live. I can only speculate as to why there was suddenly no peace, but given the history of that house of worship, I can't say that I was surprised.

Now, I'm from Toronto, Canada, did not grow up in a Christian household, and am from the hood, the West-end Jane-n-Finch neighborhood to be exact. So, I had a certain rough personality. In my past, I had a problem with anger so, I'm not gonna lie, that old mentality, lifestyle, and reaction of my past wanted all the smoke and then some. I wanted to call her so bad and speak out against that nasty spirit of manipulation that tries to control the children of God. Thank God for godly sisters in Christ that will allow you to vent, in a healthy way, but keep you in check. Whewwww. My beautiful BF was able to hear me out and allow me to get my emotions out because I felt it was so ridiculous that I wasn't able to connect with the individual on a platform that's used to lift the name of God I served.

Listen no matter what God will get the glory. A prophetic word was spoken to me to "watch who God replaces to fulfill that space." Since her refusal, there have been many amazing individuals with incredible life journeys on the show ever since. I've always said it's not about me, it's about the kingdom of God and winning souls for His glory. People need to get out of themselves and see the bigger picture that we are here to build the Kingdom.

CHAPTER 5
It Was Time to LEAVE

After ten years of dedicated service to a ministry - growing, learning, and even serving in a leadership position – I began to feel as if I was just going through the motions of church. Everything had become a repetitive routine. Church on Sunday morning and evening, mid-week service, and the bible study small group. I honestly felt like it was just something to do and started to question why I was there.

My breaking point was walking into the sanctuary during one of the church fasts and feeling as if I was there physically but spiritually disconnected. I went home that evening and had a conversation with God about my why, what was my purpose, and why was feeling this urge that there had to be more that I should be growing and learning. This was beyond the natural hunger I've always had to learn and know more when it came to God. That hunger could be fulfilled by reading various books from well-known faith-based leaders. This was definitely something more.

I went to my pastor for guidance and direction because I was feeling so disconnected. He advised me to fast and seek God regarding what I was feeling and assured me that it was only a season that I was going through and it would be alright. From that conversation, I truly thought everything would be alright. I did not expect how everything would begin to change. I was obedient to the instruction and fasted. As I was fasting, I continued to have the same feeling of something being missing in my life and walk knowing that there had to be more to this Christian walk besides going to service every Sunday morning and evening and other services during the week.

Let's fast forward. I had a dream that I was in the house of my pastor for our cell leadership group having a regular conversation as we usually did with those gatherings. I would often remain quiet and chat when I felt the need to give my input. There were eight leaders there and we eventually all moved to the dining area where I noticed the table set up was like the set-up like a scene from The Godfather. You know the set up where everyone is sitting around but there's one empty seat at the helm and it's kind of spaced away from the others. As the pastor and his wife were getting food, he began to talk about the new ministry that was coming into Toronto from America. I shared that I would be leaving the ministry to join it because I felt that this was where God was taking me.

Immediately I noticed two female leaders texting each other. In my head I was thinking, "Here we go, they are chatting about me." Everyone present had looks of concern on their faces. The pastor pointed at me and said, "You look confused. Are you sure you want to leave? Are you sure you're supposed to leave?" Feeling attacked due to the way I was questioned and yelled at after my announcement, I replied, "Yes, I am."

And then I woke up! Confused in the aftermath, I said a simple prayer that Saturday morning asking God to keep me as I would soon be leaving that church. The following Sunday I received a message after service from my Pastor requesting for me to meet him in the board room. Totally oblivious and not really thinking anything of it, I headed over to the boardroom. As I entered, my dream immediately popped back into my head. There was no godfather-style table, just a regular long office conference room-style table. I sat at the table and the pastor said that it was only fair that I told the rest of the team what was happening with me. I must admit, I was caught off guard because I was not expecting that to happen so quickly. I told everyone that I felt that God was leading me to leave the ministry to join another. I was asked if I was going into another leadership position and I responded that I was not, I would be joining as a new member. Honestly, I didn't care for a title, nor did I want to have any type of position.

It seemed as if everyone had something negative to say. The Pastor scolded me saying that's not how God does things and that we are supposed to go up, not take steps downward, referring to relinquishing my role in leadership to become a general member. His wife then questioned if I was sure that God told me to move because, during my speech to them, I said, "I think" and that made me sound confused and unsure. One leader directly said, "God never said that and that I needed to stay because my assignment was at that church, and I wasn't done yet." I left the meeting feeling confused, anxious, and a complete wreck. I mean ugly cry and all. I bumped into my best friend and told her what had just happened in the church. She was completely shocked but reminded me of the dream I had a few days prior.

I mentioned earlier that I felt the need to go and grow deeper with God. I thought maybe if I took some classes offered by the church it would help with my hunger for more. I signed up for classes and did enjoy them as I naturally love to learn and there's so much to learn about God. However, I still felt like there was more for me and the time was coming for me to leave. It's funny how a few years prior, maybe in 2014, I had a dream about attending another church where the women of God pulled me aside to tell me to stay where I am until God says to move. Mind you I had thoughts of leaving but it wasn't that strong until 2016. At that time a few church members had been attending another new church and some had left the church for the new ministry. An older lady I was close with at that time had attended a few times and told me about that particular ministry. I was called into the office by my pastor and his wife to advise that it wasn't good to attend other churches and that the massive following of some of the newer ministries was due to the pastor being involved in some level of witchcraft and that I should be careful. I informed them that although I'd been invited to attend a service there, I had no interest in going and I shared the dream I had with the women telling me to stay where I was until God said to move. The pastor said good, but I found it weird that he and his wife had a side-eye moment at the expense of my share.

In 2017, I was introduced to a ministry on YouTube and one of the teaching series blew me away. I remembered never hearing the gospel preached in that manner and being torn up in my home. I watched the entire series and began to do my research on the ministry and pastor. In doing so,

I began to feel that the ministry was legit, and the teaching seemed to be sound, so I continued to watch and learn more about them.

I noticed that everything that I wanted to learn more about was offered at that ministry. I know the Holy Spirit is the BEST teacher and we are to study to show ourselves approved, but there is a reason that teaching is a 5-fold gift, it's necessary for growth. I'm very big on going home after a service or hearing a word and searching the Bible myself for what was preached to me. The ministry held an annual conference which I thought was amazing and was super excited to attend. I made preparations to attend with two other friends. I've attended conferences in the past but for some odd reason, one of my friends told me that the pastor needed to approve and bless his members that would be traveling for another ministry's conference. I honestly thought it was completely odd because we're all one body and I know for certain that the ministry that I would be attending the conference for was a sound ministry. So, I let the pastor know that I would be attending the conference and gave the dates. I was determined to attend and had a made-up mind that no one on this earth could tell me not to go!

I attended the conference, was extremely blessed, and knew even more that I needed to be part of that ministry. When I arrived back in Toronto, I began seeking God pertaining to my move and felt it was time. I scheduled a meeting with the pastor and what I thought would have been an hour or two-hour meeting ended up being a six-hour meeting. I went into that meeting confident and ready to inform the pastor that I would be leaving the ministry only to leave confused and as if I didn't hear correctly from God. Prior to the conversation, the Pastor told me he knew that I was coming and was waiting on me to finally say something. I was like okay. I was told not to listen to that particular pastor and to talk with someone in the church. I was encouraged to speak with an individual whom I considered a spiritual mother to help me pray and she would pray for me concerning this possible move. I can honestly admit that I had never in my entire life felt that level of confusion. I felt like my head was spinning. I decided to be obedient for a little while and I didn't listen to that particular ministry and pastor preach or his messages.

Have you ever felt lost? Like you don't know whether you're coming or going or if things that you were sure of in your life made sense? Well, that's how I felt. I felt as if I didn't have a relationship with my Heavenly Father, as if I didn't know God's voice for myself, and that I had to do everything that the set man of God said to do. So, I prayed, fasted, cried, and shared my deepest thoughts and emotions with my BF. I really sought the face of God to receive clarity for myself and then for the decision. I knew that what I heard was clear and I sent the Pastor a WhatsApp message in response to him asking me what my decision was because he hadn't heard from me regarding what we spoke about. I replied by letting him know that my decision would remain the same, that I would be leaving the ministry. A week later I received a WhatsApp message from the pastor saying he is releasing me from the church and that I'm free to go. Which would follow with my dream and the team meeting within the next few days.

Little did I know that I would hear message after message about how wrong it is for people to leave a church God placed them in. I would hear another pastor say, "Just because a ministry brings in another pastor to minister, that does not give permission for any congregation members to leave and follow that person." I remember being sent recordings of sermons and teachings that it is disobedient to leave a ministry. I also sat in services hearing about people who left that particular ministry and how their lives didn't end up well. I was even encouraged to read a book entitled *Loyalty and Disloyalty*, mind you a few years back we were encouraged to read this book as one of the bible study teachings as a whole church. I had friends that I was really close with being pulled into the office to be "checked in on." I got a random DM from someone who I was close to asking for a leader's number, which was a number pretty much everyone in the youth department knew, but as we like to say and do, I "played fool to catch wise". I said whatever, gave them the number, and waited for them to send a follow-up message asking why I was leaving the church. When it came, I opened it to let them see that I saw the message and left them on read. I had one person message me saying that they heard a rumor about me leaving and wanted to know if it was true. I replied saying thanks for asking and yes, I have left the ministry. This person wanted to have a conversation with me, which I was open to, but it never happened. However, the same person who appeared to show concern invited a close friend of mine who was fairly new to the church to dinner only to try to discredit me and trash my name. Whelp, she picked the right friend because my sis let her have it.

When I finally left the church, I was bombarded with various dreams of seeing black Dobermans trying to attack me and drag me back to a house or dreams of being bitten by a Doberman. I would arrive home late in the evening only to see an owl sitting outside at the back of my house in the middle of the night. Thank God I know a thing or two about deliverance and studied demonology, so I knew these were attacks of the enemy. This went on for almost a month with wicked dreams and/or seeing animals which I knew represented monitoring spirits. I had to fast and do some serious praying to break free from word curses, any soul ties, and strongholds, as well any unforgiveness.

They did try to do a farewell dinner and wanted to bless me with a gift but I was so hurt, annoyed, and angry that I absolutely wanted nothing because I felt it wouldn't be coming from a pure place; especially after all the warfare I went through and hearing so much negative feedback and comments from close friends at that ministry during that time. It was sad because with each comment I would hear I knew just who said what and would be so disappointed. There were people I served in ministry with and thought were my friends only to be gossiped about and lied on, without one of them coming to ask me how I was doing or what really happened.

I remember attending a prayer night at the ministry with a friend I made from the new ministry. Some people greeted me while others wondered why I was there. In my head, I was thinking, "Are we not allowed to attend a church for prayers?" After that, I said I would never step foot back in that church ever again, but that was short-lived because I did so for a friend's wedding and even that was awkward as I saw some older pastors and was ignored when I said hello. At that point, I was completely over it and had actually become angry at certain church folks and hurt by a few friendships that dissolved because I left a church to attend another for my personal growth. But thank God I was able to heal through the right counsel, surrendering the situation to God, and allowing Him to heal that wound. It took a while to completely heal from the hurt caused by pastors and church members because I really did not trust anyone within the four walls of the church. I had such a deep wound that I was totally cool with attending Bedside Tabernacle and YouTube University. I did receive a WhatsApp message from the pastor wanting to talk and although I was totally open to meeting and chatting, it never happened. Even today, I'm still open to it but that would totally be a "thus says the Lord" moment. It's all love regardless! I pray nothing but blessings upon my former ministry. I will never forget all that was taught and how much I grew while there. I know without my time there I wouldn't be the woman of God I am today. I will never forget all the times I was blessed spiritually, financially, and emotionally, in addition to the support I received.

CHAPTER 6
The "Called" Can Be Haters Too

Y'all probably saw this title and thought no she didn't?! Oh yes, I did! Let's journey back to when I was a newbie, you know still fresh in the things of the Lord.

My then-boyfriend took me to his church where I attended for a few years. This was the place where I got saved. Mind you, we were still living in sin. I became really close with a lady within the church who was the wife of one of the pastors. I thought the nature of our relationship was cool. We would talk often, go out to eat, you know someone I respected and loved. I saw her as being rooted in the things of God and a married woman whom I could glean and learn a lot from. You remember I said I was saved but still living in sin, well I became pregnant with my son. We were a young couple, not married, and attending a church where my son's father practically grew up. His parents were elders of the church and I knew they didn't like a chick like me who grew up in the hood, and did not go to university or speak eloquently with their son.

We decided to have a conversation with the pastor and his wife where we revealed that I was pregnant. They prayed and gave us counsel. Wonderful right? Well shortly after I noticed a change in how the wife treated me. She became very distant and was often cold. She would ignore me and my calls or there was always some type of excuse from her for not communicating or hanging out or getting together like we used to. It was very hard for me as I really connected with her and then out of nowhere ever since I mentioned that I was pregnant everything changed. It was as if I never existed.

In prayer, it was revealed to me that the change in her behavior was because I was pregnant, and she had been unable to conceive. Wow right!? Now I know y'all might be saying, "Girl you are bold to assume and say that!" Well, it may have been bold, but it was correct as later the couple revealed they were unable to have children. Listen, you can tell when someone is upset, jealous, or bitter without the Holy Spirit. However, we cannot ignore it when our gifts are in operation and God is revealing things to us.

I think it's pretty safe to say that many of us have experienced a time when we were excited about a blessing, but someone wanted to try to steal our joy due to their jealousy and unhealed feelings. I also believe that many of us have also had the unfortunate experience of being a person who was unhealed. I know because I have been jealous and bitter before, but I praise God for healing because it is an ongoing thing to continuously keep yourself under subjection by the Holy Ghost. It is also important for us to constantly go before our Heavenly Father asking Him to wash and cleanse us from our unrighteousness for we do sin in deed and in thought, knowingly and unknowingly. It's a daily self-check, sometimes hourly! But we got this, we just gotta be real with ourselves and own up to our mess.

It's just sad that anyone would mistreat another individual in any type of way because they are not healed. Another area that many of us leaders need to be set free in is leading and bleeding. I can't tell you how many times I've had to sit myself down because I knew something was off. There have also been times when I was off and operated as a leader by laying hands, praying, etc. Yes, there's grace but at the same time, we shouldn't lead and bleed. It's so unhealthy. I remember seeing the couple a few years later and she was still very distant. No matter how many times I tried to speak or how loudly, I could have been standing directly in her line of sight, she would still ignore me. Whelp, as we know a lot of times it's the inner self that always needs lots of work and no one is exempt!

CHAPTER 7
Why Y'all Mad at What We Got On?

Where do I begin? I never really had a crazy experience with my dress code; however, I've witnessed a few friends get attacked based on something they had on.

One beautiful Sunday morning I invited my friend to church. She agreed to come and of course, I was excited. You know when you've been praying, encouraging, and working hard for those individuals and then they finally say yes!?! Listen … insert butterfly dance here! Shondo!!

I would often sit in the front row. My friend had on a black mid-thigh pencil skirt. Now y'all know, no matter what most of us ladies wear, if we got curves, they are showing! As we sat down during praise and Worship, an older lady who was known for dressing in her bright outfits, tights, skirts, heels, you name it (do your thang boo), saw my friend and walked up to me interrupting my time of praise. She leaned over to me and said, "Is that your friend?" In my head, I'm like, "Well, no duh, Batman," but I smiled and said yes. She then replied that I should take her scarf and tell her to use it to cover her legs. Then she danced back to her seat and held the scarf up for me to see it and come get it. Thankfully my friend did not see her hold up the scarf, 'cause I know that would have gone all the way left. I was so annoyed.

I totally get dressing modestly, being fashionable, and of course, always being mindful of not having body parts exposed. I was told if you can bend over and not have "Arizona" exposed you were good. But there was honestly nothing wrong with her skirt or what she had on period. I actually thought, what would have happened if I had taken the scarf and given it to her? Mind you she was just coming to the Lord and still in that early stage of wanting to know about Him. Actually, getting her to come to church was joyful by itself and she was happy to be there. It would have been a whole thing to stop her and say, "Hey take this scarf because you're sitting in the front row and your legs are showing." To a new believer, I'm sure that would have been like wait, what, why? I did speak to my friend after the incident letting her know what had happened. Thankfully she didn't get upset, she did say that it was all she had to wear and that she gets dressed in a way that's not exposing her body.

Another incident I witnessed was when my Bff and I returned for a Sunday night service. My Bff had on ripped jeans. As she was returning to our seats, she was stopped by an usher who told her that her jeans were inappropriate. I looked at her face and immediately jumped up to my feet to get her to just move away from the usher. I understand that certain styles may be revealing, however, what she had on did not fall into that category. Her jeans were only ripped at the knees. I am a strong advocate for speaking with respect to everyone no matter age, race, etc. I am also mindful in my approach, yet I find many older seasoned folks and some non-seasoned folks react abruptly and rudely in cases like what I mentioned. Too often many individuals are singled out in church at inappropriate times and spoken down to with regards to what they are wearing, or you will hear snide comments about what "sister so and so" was wearing today.

After the incident, we had a conversation about clothing and church. We both agreed that the way we once dressed would have raised eyebrows, however, now we definitely would be convicted by the Holy Ghost if we ever put something on to go anywhere before leaving the house. I truly believe this thing concerning clothing is an ongoing topic and I see nothing wrong with looking good and or wearing a certain style, however, we should be involving God in everything that we do, even our clothing and what we put on.

Let's talk about body art, tattoos to be exact. I personally don't have a problem with them as I do have a few myself. However, I know this has been a constant topic within the church body. Leviticus 19:28 NKJV says "You shall not make any cuttings in your flesh for the dead, nor tattoo any marks on you: I am the Lord." It has also been argued that we shouldn't defile our temples, (1 Corinthians 6:19-20). I agree the word is the word and I'm not about to start a huge debate, but I bring it up to say, seek God and WISE counsel. To those of us that have already been tatted, we are no less of a believer because we have them. Additionally, no one should be looked at sideways whenever they enter a church just because they have tattoos.

I do believe that individuals should be given The word in a loving manner and be prayed for and with so that they can make decisions for themselves. I'm just saying this because I know all too well that feeling of being judged because of my tattoos and I'm sure many can relate.

CHAPTER 8
The Pastor Said and Did What Now?

I'm sure we've heard of some interesting things a man or woman of God may have said whether it was on the pulpit or directly/indirectly to an individual. I know how those sermons can be direct shots.

Well, I have personally had this experience. In my early years as a believer, I served in the youth ministry. I was so on fire and full of zeal that I would've even preached to a donkey to get him saved. A friend and I were on the hospitality team for an upcoming concert. We decided to sell snacks, drinks, and patties, (a Jamaican staple which is a pastry typically filled with beef but can also have veggies, curry goat, ackee, or saltfish). We decided to order from a place different from the normal place the church used. I can hear you asking, "Why not just use what they're used to?" Well, for whatever reason, that place wasn't available to fill our order, I think they were closed.

Having no idea about church event planning and budgeting, we felt we were going for quality with the higher-priced location and since the purchase was approved, we assumed that we had done everything we needed to do. The day of the concert arrived and we did not sell a lot at all! There were so many leftovers. I felt horrible and defeated. I tried to think of every reason I could that the sales were unsuccessful. Of course, the Pastor was not happy and, in his displeasure, he called me an idiot!

Now, I'm from the streets, those are borderline fighting words. I was hurt, disappointed, and embarrassed. I nearly lost it. I knew that a lot of the failure was from poor marketing, but to be called an "idiot" for my efforts was unnecessary. Remember, I was still new in my walk, and I wanted to handle some things differently but instead, offense quickly set in, and with it came anger and bitterness.

I left the church for one year because I was highly offended. During that time, I was on a mission to let everyone I was close to know that those church folks were whack. I left the church and went back to the world. I partied, went back to drinking hard, having sex, and had a man in NYC out living "my best life." But God! He dealt with me, and I thank Him for never leaving me despite the fact I was wrong in my reaction to the situation. I thank God during my wild out period for the women of God who constantly called my phone or sent text messages asking where I was and if I was okay because it was from a genuine place. During my year away, I would often visit the church randomly once or twice a month. Each time I did, I was called into the office because one of the pastors had been asking about me and since they had seen me, they immediately sent someone to get me. After a bit of hesitation, I went to speak with the pastor. I must admit, I felt missed and cared for and about. They let the pastor know I was offended and she was willing to set up a meeting to have a conversation, unfortunately, that meeting wasn't possible but her showing that amount of concern for me as a person meant so much to me. I returned, forgave, and was able to work on forgiveness to put it past me. I never got the opportunity to sit with the pastor who actually offended me to discuss this because he was no longer there.

I share this story because I know there are many of us who can relate to something negative, disrespectful, rude, or offensive that a man or woman of God, pastor, leader, or congregation member has said. I've learned over the years that just because they have the title Pastor, Bishop, Evangelist, Apostle, or whatever doesn't mean they won't get in their flesh nor are they exempt from speaking unruly. It's just a reminder for us all, especially as we serve God's people and may be placed at a little elevated level, that it never gives us any excuse to be disrespectful. Even if what an individual has done may be more than enough grounds to pop off, (let's be honest sometimes common sense ain't common), we should always be mindful of how we respond, comment, or react.

CHAPTER 9
Inappropriate Behaviors

O nce while running a weekly Bible study group, a young lady shared with me that a pastor in the church had invited her to his home numerous times. She had not been to his home but she felt extremely uncomfortable around him because he continuously made advances at her. Once at a conference, he asked her to meet him in a private section of the church where the event was being held. She asked me to go with her because at a public event, why would you ask someone to a

73

private secluded section to talk? I went but stayed in the distance. Seeing me, he asked why I was there, and I replied because she asked me to come with her. Needless to say, he cut their conversation short. He'd also asked to see her breasts. At that point, I told her we should talk to someone, at first she was afraid. All of this concerned me because I'd experienced molestation and rape at a young age and was still in the process of healing. Having had that experience, opened me up to be a safe space for her. I prayed that the pastor would be revealed and a few weeks later he made similar attempts at another young lady, and she spoke up. Her speaking out prompted the young lady I knew to also come forward with her story. Sometime later, a sister I looked up to was talking to me about the situation and she reminded me that it is always right to speak up. To you reading this, I remind you, ALWAYS SPEAK UP.

Another woman shared with me that the reason she will not be committed to a church is that she was assaulted by a well-known pastor. When she told her mother, she was called a liar and made to feel that she was the problem. Wow! Just wow! I'm sure there are many stories of men and women being sexually assaulted by pastors, leaders, and other church members that are swept under rugs.

Obviously, God is not pleased. As the body of Christ, what are we doing about this? Where is the safe space for individuals to share and begin healing? Now I know the anointing is and can be attractive to many and there are some individuals that are specifically sent to attack the pastors, etc. However, we can't brush under the rug what is literally a Greenleaf episode/series happening before our very own eyes. We are all responsible and should never be afraid to call out sin when we see it or even if it's revealed to us. WE NEED TO EXPOSE IT!

Curses from the Saints

Can pastors, leaders, and church members **STOP** telling those who have left that church that they are going to die, their life won't be well, and they are cursed? STOP attempting to curse individuals in Jesus' name or manipulating scriptures by preaching what was shared privately and suddenly acting as if it was a word from the spirit sent to enlighten the congregation for that Sunday morning's sermon. I often question what spirit, because it does not appear to be the Holy One. It baffles me how many stories there are about hearing that people need deliverance because they are living in fear because the pastor cursed them for leaving and going to another ministry. Or they've shared something extremely private with the man or woman of God and they heard their story used as a whole sermon.

I once knew a woman who had cancer and after struggling with her illness initially, it went into remission. During that time she became a member of a new church and unfortunately, the cancer returned and she passed away. After her passing, it was stated in front of the entire congregation that the reason her cancer returned, and she ultimately passed away was because she left the church where she received healing. Her cancer coming out of remission was due to her disobedience and being out of alignment with where God had placed her.

The things that are being said to people are a complete mess. It is so important that everyone has their own personal relationship and revelational knowledge of Jesus Christ for themselves. So when the enemy attempts to arise we can use our god given authority to cancel, reject, and rebuke whatever does not align with the word of God in scripture and for one's life.

CHAPTER 10
There's Always That "One"

L et's not only talk about the negative within a church setting. I have been blessed to have a few men and women of God whom I could tell truly have a heart for God's people.

One couple, whom I adore and will forever have a place in my heart and on my prayer list, took the time to nurture me after I had left the church for a year. When I returned, they were there to really care for my soul. Talk about God's timing! The man of God, who was a youth pastor, asked me my age. At that time I was twenty-seven years old and thought I was such a big screw-up, a huge mess that God had no use for and would not use me. The man of God said in such a calm manner, "The Lord has use of you" "The Lord has what??" I thought to myself. "Huh, who me, this same chick who was in NYC last month bussin' it open for who I thought was my man? This single mama who had a child out of wedlock? This chick who used to sell weed, who loved to party, drink, and smoke? (I got more stories but I'll save them for another time). The Lord has use of me?" Still puzzled and in disbelief, I went along my little way. Well, Pastor Man did not let me go back the same way I came! He definitely was meant to help shape me into the woman of God I am blessed to be today along with his incredible wife.

I have been blessed with such wonderful individuals while serving in ministry who helped me when I literally had no money and nothing in my cupboard. I've had pastors be a major blessing to me not only spiritually but also financially. I don't ever want to be seen as someone who won't recognize the blessings that have been in my life. I am forever grateful to those who have sown into my and my son's lives, those who have labored with and for me in prayer, and those whom I wanted to fight during deliverance but still saw that I would be fully delivered.

Although some relationships dissolved, I still give credit and honor where it's due. We can't forget those who treated us well. We shouldn't ever use the excuse that since one person, or a few people, within a church body, mistreated us, we have the right to write off everyone within the church body. NO! There are true people of God with the heart of the Father and that carry the love of Jesus within the body, so I salute you all. Keep doing the Father's work and keep loving on the forsaken ones.

CHAPTER 11
I Did What Now?

Have you ever been falsely accused of something that when you were questioned about it, and even rebuked, made you shake because there was nothing you could do or say to prove yourself?

Whelp, that happened to me while I was in a particular ministry. Here I am happy to be in a new space, met some new friends, and thought, "Hey this is a nice change. Nice women I can actually be myself around, everyone seems to be on the same page, and we're all looking for fellowship." We decided to have dinner at a restaurant which was cool. So of course, there were various conversations going on, after all, we were women having dinner.

One conversation, in particular, came up about being single, single pastors within the church, and dating experiences, etc. The conversation in itself was harmless. To this day I am convinced that every person in church during their single season has at some point thought of how to date in a church, do you date from your church, and what about single pastors in a church, or divorced pastors? That was pretty much the basis of our conversation along with other sidebar conversations about hair, clothes vacations, etc. We all had a great night and went home.

A few days later I was out of the country, (Canada), and traveling to Miami, Florida for a conference, so I had no clue what was going on with church.

Apparently, while I was away it was said that I, along with the other women at the dinner, were talking negatively about the head pastor of a ministry along with other pastors. HUH?? SAY WHAT!?! Of course, I was upset beyond words. I was at the beginning of my healing journey from a lot of negative remarks placed upon my name from one ministry and here I am being accused of disrespecting a particular person of God whom I loved and respected. My sisters who traveled with me told me that they had never seen me that shaken up before. I was literally shaking and crying. Y'all, I was so annoyed to have received that type of call and felt that I couldn't properly defend myself because I was so far from home. BRUH!

When I returned to Toronto, I had a meeting with one of the Leaders to discuss what happened and made it clear that no one at the table was saying anything negative. I also felt that we should have a group meeting with all parties involved there. That never happened and a few relationships were dissolved due to speculations that one person said something to the Pastor. In spite of that, I was able to get out of my emotions, forgive, and move on as well as have a few needed conversations with some individuals to clear the air and to apologize for any mix-up. Y'all I was so confused. I'd never had to experience that level of mix-up and drama ever, especially within a church setting. Whew.

So, what do you do when there's "drama" within your church? It's easy to wonder why there is drama to start with, but the reality is that we're all humans, and whether we like it or not, we sometimes operate in our flesh. Yes, many of us can say we don't have that issue, but it is an issue within the church body, and if one is affected then it affects us all. Collectively, we all need to really look at the church and every member as a true family, instead of just saying we're family and leaving many with feelings far away from feeling like a family. I get it some individuals don't want anyone knowing their business and that's okay, but no one should ever leave a church feeling like they're alone and have no one to relate to or talk to.

CHAPTER 12
After the Heart of Who?

In regard to pastors, the Word of the Lord says in Jeremiah 3:15, "And I will give you shepherds according to My heart, who will feed you with knowledge and understanding." 1 Peter 5:1-4 follows up with instructions, "The elders who are among you I exhort, I am a fellow elder and a witness of the sufferings of Christ, and also a partaker of the glory that will be revealed: Shepherd the flock of God which is among you, serving as overseers, not by compulsion but willingly, not for dishonest gain but eagerly; and when the Chief Shepherd appears, you will receive the crown of glory that does not fade away."

The church today has changed. I agree with leadership and pastors when they say, "the Word is the Word and will never change." While this is true, there must be some type of understanding, a connection between the current world and the unchangeable Word of God. As we see there's A LOT of entertainment within the four walls of the church from public relations to smoke machines and strobe lights. I remember seeing an Instagram Reel where a young man brought his female friend out with him. You see the lights flashing, hear the music banging, and she asks him, "What club is this?" As they are both jamming, he replies that it's his church! After that you see the worship team singing "Way Maker," as the young lady stands in amazement. Now I found this hilarious, but this is a lot of what is currently seen within church settings.

You get a club-type vibe. Now I'm for praise and I love music, however, there should be a distinction. No one should walk into any house of God and question if it's a club or a church. Something is definitely wrong if that ever is the case and I wonder what we are doing with the body of Christ.

I heard an evangelist say something so intriguing, "If you preach carnal messages you have to keep them through carnal ways." I can agree with this statement that some messages that are preached don't speak about killing the flesh or living a life of holiness Such as not having sex before marriage, not giving into outbursts of rage and anger, or something that I had to really deal with, drinking alcohol as a vice to be a relaxer from a crazy day or just to drink because I need a drink to make me feel good. Nor are they about doing away with old habits that are displeasing to God, such as gossip, unforgiveness, and lying just to name a few. The truth is living in this world and in a time where because of social media everything is in your face and raw, it makes it even more difficult to live a holy life. Each of us needs to take ownership of walking out our own salvation with fear and trembling. This may include shutting off social media, and no longer engaging in certain things that can cause one to live opposite of what the Bible says, and this can also include people.

Another area that I have noticed that has been a hot topic is tithes and offerings. I have heard many say that they don't believe in giving tithes or offerings to the church because of various reasons. Many feel the church is robbing the congregation and some just say they refuse to give it. Listen, I tithe money but there are other ways one can tithe. Let's face it, I've been through a season where I had no money and was struggling and felt guilty to the point of worthlessness because it was preached that I should never come into God's presence without leaving an offering behind but I could barely rub two pennies together. I have been in conferences and regular church services where I've witnessed the pastor or guest speaker demanding nothing less than a $1000 seed offering and many times I myself have been made to feel as if I didn't give the money my life would not be blessed because I didn't or couldn't give whatever amount they requested. I've even heard a pastor say to sow a certain amount as a seed of protection. Now, we can go to God ourselves to pray and interpret scriptures such as Psalm 91 and Psalm 23 and apply the victorious Blood of Jesus. We don't ever have to sow a seed offering to any man on this earth for protection.

When we look at the ministry of Jesus Christ, we see how He was connected to the heart of the Father which was to serve and meet the needs of the people to draw their hearts to Him. Many are suffering and experiencing various levels of trauma because they feel alone. In many churches today, there seems to be a huge disconnect when it comes to truly caring for the flock that's been entrusted to the set man or woman of the house. I've personally experienced not receiving replies to messages or emails that I have sent out to Pastors. I've heard many stories of members being left on "read" by their man or woman of God which left them feeling neglected and developing a lack of trust. I've personally witnessed individuals receive promises from the pastors that they would be supported only to discover that at the time of need for counsel, the pastors were nowhere to be found. I've witnessed individuals being blocked from social media pages at the pastor's request and/or being unfollowed and unfriended when they were really good friends before. All of this is because of the Pastor's orders to the church members or because members want to be loyal servants to their pastors and do all that they say.

I often sit and think about the examples we read about Jesus. He was always for the people. Yet in today's churches, it seems to be an extreme rarity that you find men or women of God that really have a heart for the people. It's almost as if the pastor's job now is to deliver a "fire word," jump around, then leave. There's no more accountability, no checking in, or developing a strong leadership team that is the extension of the pastor. What used to be trusted leadership now appears to be built on hype and full of those who see themselves as being "better" than others because of their title.

I wonder if we are after the wrong things when we should be after the heart of the Father, which is to ensure that salvation is preached and meeting people where they are to see their total deliverance. I understand some individuals are straight-up challenging, and pastors are still human. It just seems that I see very few who truly demonstrate the Father's heart.

CHAPTER 13
We All Gotta Look Within

I've been in a few environments where I've seen individuals who were practically babies of the church their parents attended, grow up in the same church, and some of them even married there. For whatever reason, they leave the church body and then they become the topic of the next sermon, preached about, talked about, and looked down on. I've been brought into pastors' offices thinking I was being checked on only to my surprise to be questioned if I still was in contact with the individual(s) and/or warned not to attend certain other churches. I've witnessed numerous individuals leave church houses and there was absolutely no sympathy for the remaining members on how it may have affected the body. No conversations or real check-ins.

The fact of the matter is at one point or another we have all played a role in how the church body is viewed by those on the outside as well inside. It's often hard to truly see what's going on within if we don't take a step back to really examine every part, including ourselves. I know I am absolutely far from being perfect and that in this walk we all have to work out our own salvation DAILY, sometimes hourly. On the day of judgment, it will be us, individually facing our Heavenly Father, not Pastor, Bishop, Elder, Brother, or Sister.

Although we need to examine ourselves, this should be done objectively. It is possible to be so caught up in our work of ourselves that we think we are living righteously. In fact, those are probably the times when we are furthest from doing so. We're just too blind to recognize or admit that we are living in self-righteousness and not God's righteousness. Here are some questions to honestly consider in any situation:

- Am I at fault?
- Am I living in the manner that Christ has set out for me to live?
- Am I operating in pride?
- Am I being judgmental?
- Am I treating God's children right?
- Am I spreading rumors or gossiping?
- Do I think because of the "office"/ "mantle" that I'm too anointed to be checked?
- Am I cautious of the words I say to others?
- Do I think I'm too holy or righteous to believers and non-believers? How do I come across to non-believers as well as other believers?
- Do I harbor unforgiveness?
- Am I leading while bleeding?

Once we all have examined ourselves, we can turn to God the Father to ask for forgiveness. Psalm 51:17 tells us that God does not refuse a broken and contrite heart.

To anyone who was led to purchase this book, I thank you and I thank God that through His Spirit you have been led to do so. I pray that you will be healed through the precious blood of Jesus and will be able to forgive those that have hurt you. I know it will take time, however, as we see the days are really short and tomorrow definitely isn't promised. So, I ask that you rededicate yourself to God, and accept Jesus as your personal Lord and Saviour. He is the only way! Develop that relationship with Him. I pray that you will have your own revelation of who He is. Hold onto all that God has done in and throughout your life. No one can take away your testimony. We thank God for His Son and the precious blood of Jesus that has been shed for our sins.

Yes, "Church" may hurt but you don't have to carry that anymore. You are FREE!

This ride ain't easy but it sure is worth it!

-Ri

ABOUT THE AUTHOR

Richelle Milson is a native of Toronto, Canada. She is the founder of For Her Worth, where she encourages you to be all that God created you to be despite what you may have experienced in life. She is your PUSHER, dedicated to pushing you into greatness. Richelle has a background in Early Childhood Education and Social Service Work.

Richelle's favorite quote is, "This ride ain't easy, but it sure is worth it." It alludes to the fact that life is full of twists and turns, but because of Jesus, all that we go through makes it worth it!